A guide to the African Charter on human & peoples' rights

An Amnesty International Publication

First published September 1991
Amnesty International
Publications
1 Easton Street
London WC1X 8DJ
United Kingdom

AI Index: IOR 63/05/91
ISBN: 0 86210 203 0
Original language: English

Printed by:
Flashprint Enterprises Ltd.

Illustrations by:
Miles Pelo

contents

preface

This booklet is being published to mark the 10th anniversary of the adoption of the African Charter on Human and Peoples' Rights (African Charter) in 1981 and the fifth anniversary of its entry into force on 21 October 1986.

It is a guide to what your rights are under the African Charter. It explains how those rights are promoted and protected by the African Commission on Human and Peoples' Rights (African Commission) and how you can complain about violations of these rights to the African Commission.

Amnesty International has designed the booklet to suit people who are not necessarily legal or human rights experts. It complements the organization's publication and distribution in Africa of thousands of copies of the African Charter in Arabic, Bambara, English, French, Hausa, Portuguese and other African languages. Amnesty International members will also send thousands of copies of this booklet in a range of languages to educational institutions, human rights and community groups, churches, journalists and others all over Africa.

1 introduction

WHAT ARE 'RIGHTS' AND 'FREEDOMS'?

Every human being has certain fundamental rights which governments must uphold and respect. This concept is rooted in most of the world's religions and cultures and is reflected in many legal systems. It is based on the belief that all people, wherever they live, have the same basic needs.

Fundamental rights and freedoms that are universally recognized have developed over the decades. Today, these include:

- the right to life
- freedom from slavery
- freedom from torture
- the right not to face discrimination because of racial or ethnic origin, or religion
- the right not to be arrested and imprisoned arbitrarily
- the right to fair trial
- freedom of expression
- freedom of thought, conscience and religion

Agreement on what these basic rights should be

was reached by many countries in 1948 when the United Nations (UN) General Assembly adopted the Universal Declaration of Human Rights. It stated:

"...recognition of the inherent dignity and of the equal and inalienable rights of all members of the human family is the foundation of freedom, justice and peace in the world..."

At the time of this Declaration, only two African countries were not under European rule and were members of the UN — Ethiopia and Liberia. The only other country in Africa represented at the UN was South Africa.

Since then, however, the rights recognized by the Universal Declaration of Human Rights have been added to and further defined by the entire world community in treaties and standards adopted by the UN or at a regional level by the Organization of African Unity (OAU) and other similar organizations. Contributing to this process were many of the formerly colonized countries in Africa and elsewhere which had previously been denied a voice in defining the nature of rights and freedoms.

One of the regional treaties to emerge was the African Charter, drawn up in 1981 by African countries through their collective body, the OAU.

All these declarations and treaties reinforce the universally held belief that every government is obliged to protect the rights of the people within its borders. However, we know from experience that this does not always happen. It is therefore up to the international community as a whole to protect these rights on behalf of people all over the world, and it was for this reason that Amnesty International was founded.

WHY AMNESTY INTERNATIONAL IS PRODUCING THIS BOOKLET

Governments are much less likely to violate human rights if ordinary people know what their rights are and what they can do if these rights are not respected. This is recognized by the African Charter, which says that governments have a duty to inform people of their rights through education and publicity. However, lack of resources and political will have left this duty largely unfulfilled. The African Commission, which monitors the implementation of the Charter, also has limited funds. It has therefore welcomed Amnesty International's help in informing people in Africa of their rights and promoting an understanding of the African Charter by distributing the Charter and producing a booklet explaining it.

This booklet has been prepared and published by Amnesty International: the organization bears sole responsibility for its contents and for all interpretations given to the various rights and duties which are mentioned. It is not meant to be an official legal interpretation of all the rights. Rather, it explains these rights so that they can be understood by people who are not lawyers or human rights experts.

AMNESTY INTERNATIONAL'S WORK IN AFRICA

Amnesty International has campaigned against human rights violations in Africa since the organization was formed in 1961. Its members in Africa have also been working to develop a strong human rights movement in the continent.

Amnesty International members campaigned vigorously for the release of prisoners of conscience held for calling for majority rule or independence in countries which have since gained their independence, such as Angola and what was formerly Southern Rhodesia. Members around the world have continued to campaign for the release of prisoners of conscience held in South Africa because of their opposition to *apartheid*. They have also worked to end other human rights violations in South Africa, such as the torture of prisoners and the death penalty.

Women and children waiting to receive medical attention: under the African Charter governments promise to protect and promote the health of their people

© Oxfam

Similar campaigns have been directed at almost every other government in Africa in the past 30 years. Sadly, the end of colonialism did not mean the end of human rights violations.

In recent years awareness of human rights issues and interest in organizations such as Amnesty International have grown throughout Africa. Numerous leagues and other organizations have been formed by Africans at a local level to defend human rights in their home countries. Some of these are based on particular professions, such as lawyers' human rights groups, but many encourage participation by anyone who is interested.

By 1991, Amnesty International had national sections in seven African countries: Côte d'Ivoire, Ghana, Mauritius, Nigeria, Sierra Leone, Tanzania and Tunisia (see inside back cover for contact addresses). It also had smaller local groups in five other countries: Algeria, Benin, Egypt, Senegal and Zambia. This means that over 100 groups of people in Africa meet on a regular basis within the framework of Amnesty International alone to discuss human rights and campaign to stop violations all around the world.

Amnesty International hopes that the publication of this booklet will help its members and other human rights activists in Africa and elsewhere in their campaigns to end human rights violations in Africa once and for all.

2 what is the African Charter?

THE ORIGINS OF THE CHARTER

In the 1960s and 1970s several conferences were organized in Africa by the UN, African governments and non-governmental organizations to discuss an African system to promote and protect human rights. The discussions reflected the frustration felt by many Africans about the OAU, which loudly condemned human rights violations by white-ruled governments in Africa but was virtually silent about similar abuses committed in other parts of the continent.

This frustration was expressed by Uganda's President Yoweri Museveni at an OAU summit meeting in the 1980s: "While Ugandans perished...the rest of the world kept largely silent.... Ugandans felt a deep sense of betrayal that most of Africa kept silent."

He added that the lack of reaction by African states to human rights violations by other African states "tends to undermine our moral authority to condemn the excesses of others, especially South Africa's racist regime. Tyranny is colour-blind and should be no less reprehensible because it is perpetrated by one of our kind."

In 1979 the OAU Assembly of Heads of State and Government (OAU Assembly) decided that the OAU Secretary General should begin the process of establishing a regional commission on human rights. Two years later the OAU Assembly unanimously adopted the final text of the African Charter.

THE CHARTER AS A HUMAN RIGHTS STANDARD

The Charter is a set of rules, called Articles, guaranteeing certain fundamental rights of individuals. It also guarantees certain rights of entire peoples. African states which sign the Charter must obey these rules, respect Africa's traditions and moral values, and work for African unity.

The Charter is a treaty. When a state ratifies a treaty (that is, agrees to be bound by it), it becomes a State Party to it. It is then legally obliged to protect the rights specified in the treaty. States which have signed but not yet ratified a treaty have promised not to commit acts which would defeat the purpose of that treaty until such time as they decide to ratify it.

At the beginning of 1991, Amnesty International knew of only 10 of the 51 OAU member states which had not ratified the Charter:

Côte d'Ivoire
Djibouti
Ethiopia
Kenya
Lesotho
Madagascar
Mauritius
Namibia
The Seychelles
Swaziland

This means that the following 41 OAU states have already agreed to be legally bound by the Charter and to fulfil all its provisions:

Algeria
Angola
Benin
Botswana
Burundi
Burkina Faso
Cameroon
Cape Verde
Central African Republic
Chad
Comoros
Congo
Egypt
Equatorial Guinea
Gabon
Gambia
Ghana
Guinea
Guinea-Bissau
Liberia
Libya
Malawi
Mali
Mauritania
Mozambique
Niger
Nigeria
Rwanda
Sahrawi Arab Democratic Republic
São Tomé and Príncipe
Senegal
Sierra Leone
Somalia
Sudan
Tanzania
Togo
Tunisia
Uganda
Zaire
Zambia
Zimbabwe

Many of the fundamental rights in the African Charter are the same as those contained in other international standards adopted by the UN, including the Universal Declaration of Human Rights. As members of the UN, all African states, even if they have not ratified the Charter, have generally accepted that these internationally recognized standards should be observed by all countries of the world.

Several international human rights treaties also exist which protect people in all parts of the world. Among the most important are:

- the International Covenant on Civil and Political Rights and its two Optional Protocols
- the International Covenant on Economic, Social and Cultural Rights
- the Convention against Torture and Other Cruel, Inhuman or Degrading Treatment or Punishment
- the Convention on the Prevention and Punishment of the Crime of Genocide
- the Convention relating to the Status of Refugees and its 1967 Protocols
- the International Convention on the Elimination of All Forms of Racial Discrimination
- the Convention on the Elimination of All Forms of Discrimination against Women

The African Charter is similar to two other regional treaty-based systems which promote and protect human rights:

- the European Convention on Human Rights and Fundamental Freedoms (in force since 1953)
- the American Convention on Human Rights (in force since 1978)

There are, in addition, many international human rights standards which are not in the form of treaties. Most of these have been developed by the UN: any states which are members of the UN are therefore expected to follow the rules of these standards, although they are not legally binding in the same way as a treaty is. The standards include:

- the UN Standard Minimum Rules for the Treatment of Prisoners
- the UN Body of Principles for the Protection of All Persons under Any Form of Detention or Imprisonment
- the UN Economic and Social Council Safeguards guaranteeing protection of the rights of those facing the death penalty

DISTINCTIVE FEATURES OF THE AFRICAN CHARTER

The committee which drafted the Charter was guided by the principle that "it should reflect the African conception of human rights, [and] should take as a pattern the African philosophy of law and meet the needs of Africa." It also recognized the value of international human rights standards that many African countries had already promised to respect.

As a result, the Charter sets out to combine the specific needs and values of African cultures with standards that have been recognized as universally valid.

One of the Charter's distinctive features is that it recognizes the rights of peoples, such as the right of all peoples to self-determination. The exact definition of "peoples" has been left to the African Commission, which will determine whether the term means ethnic groups or other communities

A refugee being greeted on return from exile: one of the distinctive features of the African Charter is that it gives people fleeing persecution the right to seek and obtain asylum

© Christian Aid//Guy Tillim

within a state or the entire people in an existing state or territory.

The Charter is also unique in emphasizing the duties of the individual towards the community and the state, and for giving people fleeing persecution the right not just to seek asylum, but also to obtain it.

MONITORING THE IMPLEMENTATION OF THE CHARTER

Implementation of the Charter is monitored by the African Commission. The Commission is made up of 11 members, who are nominated by States Parties and then elected by the entire OAU Assembly. The members serve for six years in their personal capacities rather than as representatives of their governments.

The Commission has six main areas of responsibility:

- ensuring the protection of the rights and duties covered by the African Charter
- interpreting what the Charter says
- examining complaints made by one State Party against another
- examining complaints submitted by individuals and non-governmental organizations against states which have ratified the Charter
- promoting human rights through education and publicity
- developing principles and rules to further the protection of human rights

The Charter also directs the Commission to "draw inspiration" from international law on human and peoples' rights. The Commission should refer, for example, to the OAU and UN Charters, the Universal Declaration of Human Rights, and other African and international standards. It should also take into consideration international treaties such as the International Covenant on Civil and Political Rights when determining principles of law. This is important because for some human rights issues, other international treaties and standards offer greater protection than the African Charter.

RIGHTS AND DUTIES COVERED BY THE AFRICAN CHARTER

Four main categories of rights and duties are covered by the African Charter:

- **Individual rights**
  These are the rights you have as an individual. They include the right to life, the right not to be tortured, the right not to be arrested for no good reason, the right to a fair trial, and the right to believe what you like, write and speak freely and join organizations such as trades unions and political parties if you want to.
- **Rights of peoples**
  These refer to the rights of entire peoples to determine how they are governed and how their economies and cultures are developed.
- **Duties of states**
  These are the responsibilities of governments to protect the welfare of their citizens. They include guaranteeing the

© Oxfam/Chris Johnson

All states are obliged by the Charter to promote an awareness of human rights

independence of the law courts and promoting awareness of human rights.

- **Duties of individuals**
  These are the duties everyone has to protect and promote the welfare of all. Under the Charter they include the duty to work for your community and not to undermine the security of the state.

In the following chapters these four categories of rights and duties are outlined and explained in detail. The key Articles of the Charter referred to in the text are reproduced in their original wording on pages 60 to 66.

© Oxfam

Children playing an educational game: the African Charter protects the rights of everyone and prohibits all forms of racial discrimination

3 individual rights

EQUAL TREATMENT FOR ALL

The Charter says that everyone has equal rights and freedoms. This means it is illegal for the state to discriminate against you for any of the following reasons: *Articles 2 and 3*

- your racial or national origin
- your ethnic group, tribe or clan
- the colour of your skin
- your sex (whether you are male or female)
- the language or dialect you speak
- your religion
- your opinions or political beliefs
- your social class or how rich or poor you are
- your status at birth, such as whether your parents were married

It also means that the authorities must offer the same protection to everyone. It is therefore illegal for the police or law courts to treat people differently because, for instance, they have different racial origins or religious views, or because they are rich or poor.

THE RIGHT TO LIFE

Article 4 The Charter says that everyone is entitled to respect for his or her life and safety. It also states that no one may be arbitrarily deprived of their right to life.

This means that police officers or soldiers may not resort to lethal force — such as firing live ammunition at people — unless their own lives or the lives of others are in immediate danger and less extreme measures would not avert the danger.

To make sure this right is respected, governments must indicate clearly to soldiers and others armed with lethal weapons *when and in what circumstances* they are allowed to use their weapons. For example, soldiers and police officers must be forbidden from firing on peaceful demonstrators who are waving placards and shouting anti-government slogans — even if the government has banned the demonstration.

This right also means that in states which have not yet abolished the death penalty prisoners may never be executed without a fair trial. A fair trial includes the right to appeal and the right to apply for a reduction in sentence or a pardon. Similarly, soldiers or police hunting suspects may never kill villagers or others just because they believe they are helping rebels or criminals, or in reprisal attacks on entire communities.

Some people, including all members of Amnesty

International, interpret the right to life to mean that nobody should ever be sentenced to death or executed — even prisoners who have been found guilty in fair trials of committing serious crimes.

YOUR DIGNITY IS YOUR RIGHT

The Charter says that it is your right to have your human dignity respected. It specifically forbids any form of slavery, and no one may be "pawned" or sold into bondage. *Article 5*

The Charter prohibits torture and all forms of cruel, inhuman or degrading punishment and treatment. This means that there are no circumstances which justify the police or soldiers hurting or humiliating anyone using methods such as:

- torturing prisoners or subjecting them to beatings or other pain in order to make them "confess" or to punish them
- raping prisoners or subjecting them to sexual humiliation
- beating suspected criminals after their arrest (only reasonable force may be used to detain a suspected criminal who resists arrest)
- denying prisoners food or water to make them cooperate or "confess"

It also means that certain types of punishment practised in the past and still used in some countries are prohibited, such as:

- amputations (for example, cutting off hands or feet)

- any mutilation of the human body
- "corporal punishment", such as whipping, flogging or caning

The Charter also says you have certain rights because of your legal status. For example, you may be entitled to certain special rights or protection if you have a minor (a person under a certain age, which is 18 years under many international laws) or

because you are married. Thus, under your national law you may have the right to primary education and support from your parents because you are a minor. Husbands and wives may have certain rights to inherit property from each other simply because they are married.

RIGHT TO LIBERTY

Article 6

The Charter guarantees in broad terms the right to liberty and security. No one may be arbitrarily arrested on a criminal charge or arbitrarily detained on other grounds.

This means that women and men may only be deprived of their liberty if the authorities respect the law when doing so. The "law" means not only the national law but also implicitly refers to the internationally recognized rights contained in human rights treaties and standards (such as those cited on pages 10 and 11).

These rights include:

- the right to be informed at the time of arrest of the reasons for arrest and to be promptly informed of the charges
- the right of detainees to be brought promptly before a judge or other judicial officers
- the right to be tried within a reasonable time or released
- the right to go to a court to challenge the lawfulness of the detention

In practice, this means:

- the police or others in authority may only arrest you on a criminal charge if they genuinely suspect that you have committed a crime
- the police or others in authority may not detain you indefinitely after arrest on a criminal charge or after detention on some other ground; you must be brought promptly before a judge

In some African countries national law requires suspects to be brought before a court or an official linked to a court such as a public prosecutor within a few days. But in many of these countries arbitrary detention occurs when the authorities ignore these legal time limits. In other countries, arbitrary detention occurs because the law itself allows the authorities to keep people in detention without being brought before a court or an appropriate official for 30 days or more.

In several countries the head of state or government

ministers are allowed by national law to impose detention orders which by-pass the courts and authorize them to order the detention of certain people. This is forbidden by the Charter if the detainees do not have a right to find out why they are detained or are not given an opportunity to challenge their detention in a way which guarantees that innocent people cannot be kept in prison.

THE RIGHT TO FAIR TRIAL

Basic fair trial guarantees are contained in the Charter as part of everyone's general right to have his or her cause heard. Anyone arrested on a criminal charge has these rights, *however serious the charges against them*. In some countries the authorities believe that people accused of serious offences such as terrorism, treason or murder should lose these rights. However, the Charter allows for no such exceptions. *Article 7*

The rights and fair trial guarantees contained in the Charter include:

- the right to be presumed innocent until proper court proceedings have proved otherwise
- the right to defend yourself and to choose your own lawyer to defend you if you wish
- the right to be tried within a reasonable time: this means you may not be detained indefinitely on a criminal charge
- the right not to be convicted for an act which was not recognized by the law as a criminal offence at the time it was committed

- the right not to be punished for an offence committed by another member of your family or clan: this means the police are not allowed to arrest a relative of someone who has run away in the hope of punishing the person indirectly or forcing the person to surrender

The Charter prohibits unfair trials

- the court must be competent: this means it must have been previously established by law rather than, for example, by a special tribunal set up after the offence was committed

- the court must be impartial: the judges may not be biased — as they might be if they were members of the ruling party and the accused was an opponent of the government, or if they were military officers and the accused was a civilian
- the courts must be independent: this means, for example, that the government may not remove a judge on the grounds that he or she has acquitted a defendant

The Charter does not spell out the full scope of the right to a fair trial. Other international treaties and agreements, however, make clear that the right also includes:

- the right to a public hearing (subject to certain limited exceptions such as cases which might genuinely reveal military secrets if heard in public)
- the right to have adequate time and facilities to prepare the defence's case
- the right to be present at your own trial
- the right to free legal assistance where necessary in the interests of justice
- the right to examine witnesses
- the right to have the free assistance of an interpreter in court if necessary
- the right not to be compelled to testify against yourself either in making statements during your trial or in pre-trial detention while being interrogated
- the right to appeal to a higher tribunal

The language of the Charter suggests that these internationally recognized components of the right to a fair trial are implicit in the right to have one's cause heard. It is hoped that the Commission will interpret the Charter accordingly.

FREEDOM OF CONSCIENCE

Article 8 The Charter says that everyone has the right to freedom

of conscience. This includes the right to hold the religious beliefs of your choice. It also says that you have the right to profess and practice your religion publicly.

The Charter prohibits all governments from restricting these rights, except when it is necessary to maintain law and order. A legitimate restriction of practices which some might justify as "religious" would be, for example, the prohibition of ritual murder.

In several African countries, however, the authorities have restricted some religious denominations on the grounds that their beliefs or practices are illegal or jeopardise national unity. In many cases these restrictions have been politically motivated and constitute a violation of the right to freedom of religion. For example, certain religious denominations or sects have been restricted because they have refused to join a political party, particularly in one-party states, or have ignored government orders to perform certain rituals (such as singing the national anthem) on the grounds that they contradict religious beliefs.

Such restrictions are not allowed by the Charter. Moreover, international treaties and standards make clear that the state may *never* restrict your right to freedom of conscience no matter how extreme the circumstances and may only restrict your right to profess and practice your religion when it is absolutely necessary to do so in order to protect the public safety, order, health or morals or fundamental rights and freedoms of others.

Freedom of conscience means that you may change your religion. The state may not punish you for converting to another religion.

Freedom of conscience also means that you may refuse to fight or join the armed forces on account of your conscientiously held beliefs or religion. This right is particularly important in countries where the law says that all young men (and sometimes young women) must perform military service.

FREEDOM OF EXPRESSION

The Charter says that everyone has the right to receive information and that this right cannot be restricted in any way. It also says that everyone may express themselves in any manner they like about any subject they choose: they are allowed to tell others their opinions using any method they wish (such as in conversations, speeches and letters or through newspapers, radio or television), provided they do so "within the law". *Article 9*

To determine what restrictions governments are allowed to impose on the right to free expression, the Commission will look at international standards. These only allow restrictions which are necessary to protect the rights or reputations of others, or are needed to safeguard national security, public order, public health or morals.

This means governments are not allowed to punish people for criticizing official policies or for calling for a different form of government. It means too that the authorities should not prevent people from expressing their views by censoring newspapers or writing. The authorities should not use laws, such as those concerning sedition (inciting others to rebel), against journalists or others who simply criticize government policies or publish well-documented accounts of corruption in government circles.

It may, however, be legitimate for the parliament to pass a law permitting a person to sue someone else for libel or slander (writing or saying something false about someone else which injures that person's reputation or livelihood). It may also be legitimate for a government to prosecute someone for revealing the location of secret military installations.

However, many governments in Africa have imposed restrictions which far exceed those which are internationally recognized as legitimate. As a result, many people have been arrested and imprisoned for exercising their right to free expression, particularly after criticizing the government or producing political pamphlets.

FREEDOM OF ASSOCIATION

Article 10 The Charter says that everyone has the right to form societies and other associations, as long as they respect the law. This right covers all types of groups that do not intend to break the law, including political, trade union, religious, cultural and clan or regional-based organizations.

The Charter does not state what legal restrictions on this right are allowed. However, international standards only allow restrictions to be imposed which are in accordance with the law and are necessary in a democratic society to protect national security, public safety and order, public health and morals, and the rights and freedoms of others.

This right does not, therefore, mean that criminals may form an "association" or gang to carry out robberies, or that people may form political groups whose aims include racial murders.

Many governments have violated the right to association by, for example, banning peaceful political organizations, forbidding workers from forming trade unions, or refusing without a legitimate reason to give authorization for their associations. Often this has been done for political reasons to prevent opposition groups from organizing or to suppress the cultural or political aspirations of ethnic, tribal or religious groups.

Freedom of association also means that people may not be forced to join a political party, as they often have been required to do in one-party states.

© Oxfam/Kelvin Jenkins

Everyone has the right to demonstrate peacefully and express their views publicly

FREEDOM OF ASSEMBLY

Article 11 The Charter says that everyone has the right to meet other people and assemble freely, in private or public. It allows governments to restrict this right only when the restrictions are absolutely necessary and are imposed according to the law, such as those protecting national security, public morals, health and safety, and the rights and freedoms of others.

This means that all people have the right to hold meetings on any issue they choose provided the purpose is not, for example, to incite racial violence. It also means that everyone has the right to join or organize a peaceful demonstration, even if the protest is against the government. If the authorities effectively prevent people from demonstrating by requiring authorization which is then withheld for political reasons, they are violating people's right to assemble.

The right to assemble has often been abused by governments and security officials. Demonstrations and meetings have frequently been banned because they were organized by an opposition political party. This goes far beyond the right of the authorities to place restrictions on assemblies: the restrictions must be clearly explained in the law and based on a limited number of specific considerations, such as national security. When governments interpret "national security" so widely that every meeting of any political nature is banned, then they are violating this fundamental human right.

THE RIGHT TO TRAVEL AND TO SEEK ASYLUM

Article 12 The Charter says everyone may move about freely within their country. The authorities are allowed to restrict this right only in exceptional circumstances, such as war, when they may temporarily forbid people from leaving their home towns, for example.

Everyone may also travel freely to and from their own country, as long as they have the required travel documents. Restrictions on this right are only allowed if they are within the law and are necessary to protect national security, law and order, public health or morals.

Many governments prevent suspected opponents from leaving their country by refusing them travel documents or confiscating their passports. This may not be done unless the grounds on which it is authorized are based strictly on national security or other legitimate considerations and the factors which are taken into account are made explicit in law, so they can be challenged before the courts.

Under the Charter everyone who is persecuted has the right to ask for and obtain asylum. This means that border police or other authorities may not refuse entry to people seeking refuge, or force them to return to their own country without giving proper consideration to their request for asylum.

In addition, governments may not return refugees or asylum-seekers to countries where they risk serious human rights violations. Governments are not allowed to expel any foreigner who is legally in the country except in accordance with a decision taken by a court following proper procedures. They are also not allowed under the Charter to expel large numbers of refugees, ethnic or racial groups, or foreigners to other countries. This right covers people whose nationality is disputed by the authorities.

© UN/M Grant

A Namibian woman holds her voter registration card

THE RIGHT TO PARTICIPATE IN ONE'S GOVERNMENT

Article 13

The Charter says that everyone has the *political* right to choose their government. This implicitly means that governments should be chosen by some form of democratic process, rather than imposed as a result of a military coup or other violent means. Military governments or others which take power through force must therefore quickly prepare for handing over to an elected government within a reasonable period.

The Charter also says there must be equal access to public services for everyone. This right is aimed at preventing corruption. It means that public servants are forbidden from showing favouritism to people because of their ethnic origin or other such reason, or because they have received money or goods.

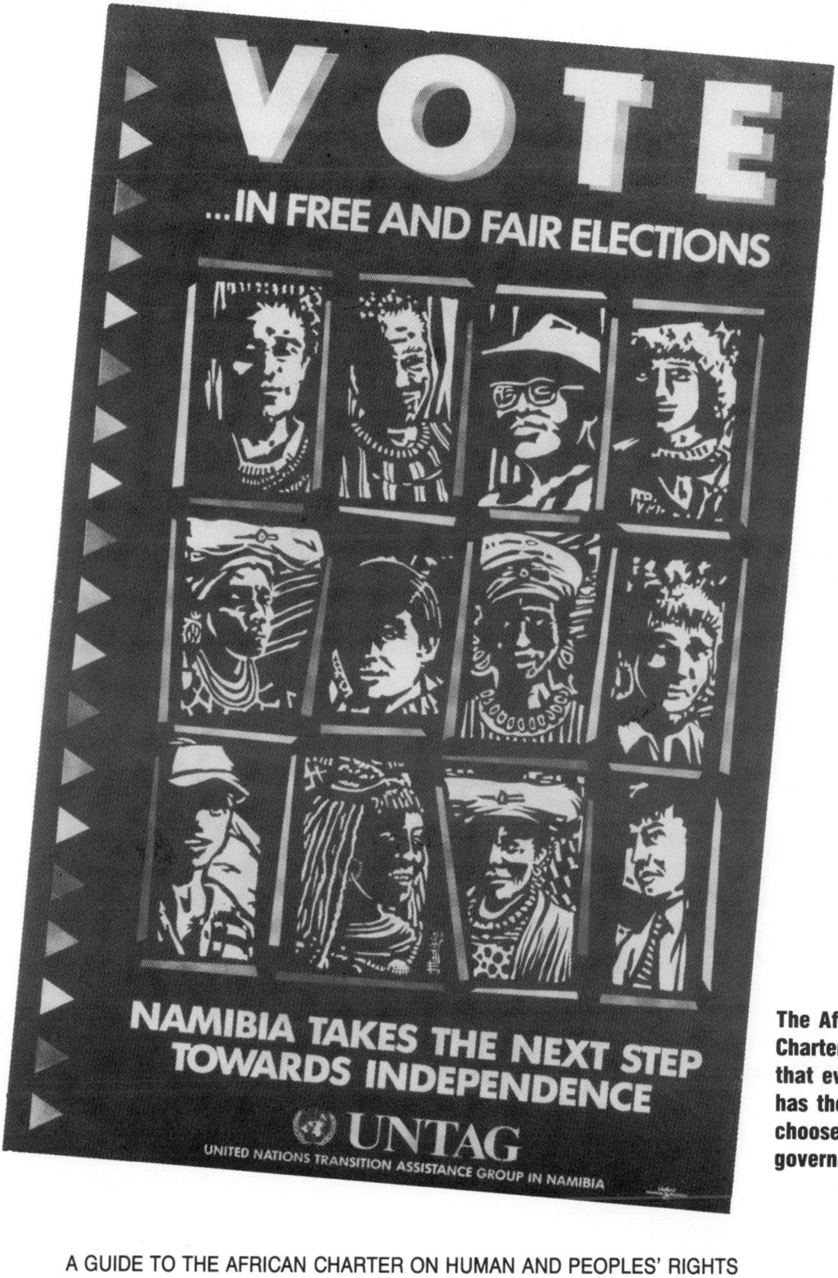

The African Charter says that everyone has the right to choose their government

ECONOMIC, SOCIAL AND CULTURAL RIGHTS

Articles 14 to 18

The Charter recognizes important economic, social and cultural rights. It also places special duties on the state to protect and promote these rights.

- **Property**
  Everyone has the right to own property, whether it be a cooking pot, a farm or a factory. This right may only be restricted for the good of the community and in accordance with the law. For example, a government may appropriate someone's land for an essential public building, giving the owner adequate compensation.

- **Work**
  Everyone has the right to work under

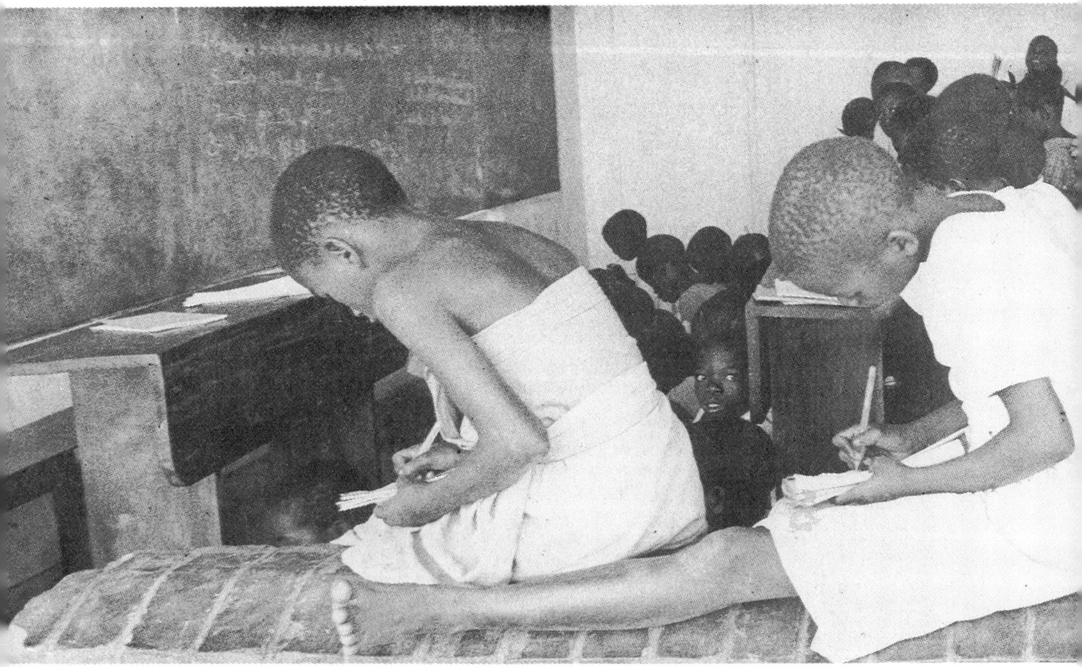

© Julia Martin

satisfactory conditions. This means employers must ensure healthy and safe working conditions. The Charter states clearly that there must be equal pay for equal work.

- **Health**
  Governments must take certain measures to protect everyone's health and to ensure that all people, including those with no money, receive adequate medical care if they become ill.

- **Education**
  Everyone has the right to education and to participate freely in the cultural life of his or her community. The Charter says that governments must promote and protect the

Everyone has a right to education

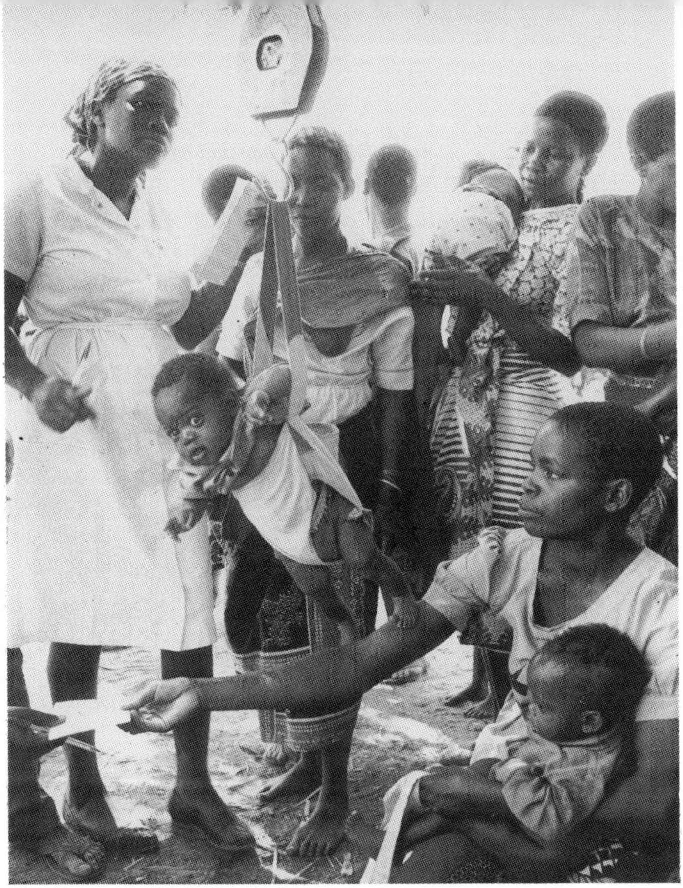

A mobile clinic checks the health of mothers and babies: under the Charter governments promise to protect the rights of women and children

morals and traditional values recognized by the community. However, the Commission still has to interpret this duty in harmony with other rights recognized by the Charter.

- **The family**
  The Charter recognizes the family as the natural unit and basis of society, which must be protected by the state. It also says that governments have the duty to end all discrimination against women, protect the rights of women and children in accordance with international declarations and conventions, and give special protection to the elderly and disabled.

4 peoples' rights

The Charter is unique among human rights treaties in that it recognizes the rights of entire peoples. This means:

Articles 19 to 24

- all peoples are equal and entitled to the same respect and rights
- there are no circumstances that justify the domination or oppression of one people by another
- all peoples have the right to exist, to self-determination and to choose their political status
- all peoples may pursue their economic and social development according to any principles they choose

Colonized and oppressed peoples therefore have the right to free themselves using any internationally recognized means. The Charter gives peoples the right to take up arms to liberate themselves from foreign domination, as long as they abide by international humanitarian standards such as not attacking innocent civilians. It also says that all such struggles must be supported and aided by other African states which have ratified the Charter.

All peoples have economic rights under the Charter. They have the right to prevent the wealth and natural resources of their country being exploited by foreigners. They also have the right to use their wealth for the good of the people as a whole and to strengthen African unity. For example, the Charter gives peoples the right to set up trade agreements to protect and develop their wealth.

All peoples are entitled to other more general rights under the Charter, such as the right to economic, social and cultural development, national and international peace and security, and a safe environment.

This means, for example, that all peoples have the right not to have their air or water supplies polluted by others, and that their land may not be used for other peoples' wars. Their land must also not be used as a base for subversive or terrorist activities against the people of any other African state which has ratified the Charter. The definition of "subversive" activities, however, must be consistent with the Charter's guarantees of freedom of conscience, religion, expression, opinion, association and assembly.

5 duties of states

Articles 1, 25 and 26

States have several duties under the African Charter. Most importantly, each must recognize the rights, duties and freedoms contained in the Charter and adopt legislative or other measures to give effect to them. In practice, however, many states which have ratified the Charter have yet to do this.

All states have the duty to promote the rights contained in the Charter and ensure respect for them, through education and publicity. They must also guarantee the independence of courts and allow national human rights organizations to develop.

> *'The member states of the Organization of African Unity, parties to the present Charter, shall recognize the rights, duties and freedoms enshrined in the Charter...'* (Article 1)

© Oxfam/Keith Bernstein

The African Charter says that everyone must preserve the harmonious development of the family

6 duties of individuals

The Charter says that everyone has certain duties towards the community and state, and that each person must exercise his or her rights and freedoms without damaging the rights of others. This reflects the importance of the community in African society.

Articles 27 to 29

The Charter states that your individual duties to the community include:

- treating others "without discrimination"
- preserving "the harmonious development of the family"
- working in the best way you can
- paying taxes imposed according to law
- preserving and strengthening "positive African cultural values" in a "spirit of tolerance, dialogue and consultation"
- promoting African unity

The Charter states that your duties to the state are:

- not to undermine national security

- to preserve and strengthen social and national solidarity
- to preserve and strengthen the national independence and territorial integrity of your country and contribute to its defence in accordance with the law

It is clear that these duties are intended to complement — not contradict — the various rights of individuals recognized by the Charter. In particular, the duty to contribute to national defence "in accordance with law" must be qualified by the right to freedom of conscience and religion.

© Julia Martin

Under the African Charter, everyone should contribute to their community in the best way they can

7 the African Commission

HOW THE COMMISSION WORKS

Articles 30 to 62

The African Commission, which monitors the implementation of the African Charter, was established in July 1987 at the 23rd session of the OAU Assembly of Heads of State and Government held in Addis Ababa, Ethiopia. It is based in Banjul, the Gambia. Its working languages are Arabic, English and French. The rules which govern the organization and operation of the Commission were adopted in Dakar, Senegal in February 1988. The Commission has appointed a working group to review the rules with a view to amending them.

The Commission's 11 elected members are "chosen from amongst African personalities of the highest reputation, known for their high morality, integrity, impartiality and competence in matters of human and peoples' rights; particular consideration being given to persons having legal experience" (*Article 31*). Members are nominated by States Parties to the Charter but elected by the entire OAU Assembly of Heads of State and Government (*Article 33*) to serve six-year terms (*Article 36*) in their personal capacities rather than as representatives of their governments (*Article 31*). At the first election in 1987, four members of the Commission were elected for two years and three for four years to avoid the entire Commission being re-elected at the same time every six years (*Article 36*). Members are eligible for re-election (*Article 36*).

The Commission normally holds two ordinary sessions each year, one in March or April and the other in October. The Chairperson of the Commission may call extraordinary sessions in consultation with other members of the Commission. The sessions are held in different countries in Africa.

In practice, the agenda for a session is based on proposals made by the Secretary and Chairperson of the Commission. In addition, any of the following may make proposals to be included in the agenda:

- members of the Commission
- the OAU Assembly of Heads of State and Government
- States Parties to the Charter
- liberation movements recognized by the OAU and non-governmental organizations

The Commission may invite any State Party or national liberation movement recognized by the OAU to participate, with a vote, in discussions of interest to them. Representatives of intergovernmental organizations granted observer status by the OAU and of non-governmental organizations granted observer status by the African Commission may participate, without a vote, in discussions of interest to them. Amnesty International was in the first group of non-governmental organizations to be granted observer status by the Commission.

At first, the sessions were held in private, except for the opening and closing ceremonial meetings. Now, all sessions are open to observers except when considering matters such as communications (complaints) about a State Party. Amnesty International has attended sessions and participated in discussions of matters within its mandate.

After each session the Commission publishes a communiqué summarizing the discussion. It prepares an annual report of its activities, which is published after approval by the OAU Assembly of Heads of State and Governments (*Article 59*).

PROMOTING HUMAN RIGHTS

The African Commission is mandated to promote human rights in the following ways:

Articles 45 and 59

- interpreting the African Charter at the request of a State Party, OAU institution or "an African organization recognized by the OAU" (*Article 45(3)*)
- undertaking studies, organizing conferences and distributing information to promote human rights (*Article 45(1)(a)*)
- encouraging national and local institutions concerned with human rights (*Article 45(1)(a)*)
- developing principles and rules aimed at solving legal problems relating to human rights, upon which governments may base their legislation (*Article 45(1)(b)*)
- undertaking any other tasks entrusted to it by the OAU Assembly of Heads of State and Government (*Article 45(4)*)

Commission members have actively promoted the Charter in several other ways. In 1990, for example, each member went to several different African countries to meet government officials, non-governmental organizations and members of the public to urge states which had not ratified the Charter to do so and those which had to implement it.

The Commission has also campaigned for all OAU member states to observe **21 October** each year as the African Day of Human and Peoples' Rights — the day the Charter entered into force in 1986.

PROTECTING HUMAN RIGHTS

Articles 46 to 62

The Commission has several important powers to protect human rights:

- **Investigations**
  The Commission has broad powers to investigate human rights issues and concerns (*Article 46*). These include hearing from the OAU's Secretary General or "any person capable of enlightening it".

- **Review of Periodic Reports**
  The Commission reviews periodic reports, which States Parties are required to submit under *Article 62* every two years, on legislative and other measures they have taken to implement the Charter. Many governments, however, have not submitted the required reports. Non-governmental organizations such as Amnesty International have submitted background information to assist the Commission in conducting its review of reports and the Commission has

questioned representatives of governments which have submitted reports.

- **Examination of State Communications**
The Commission may review communications (complaints) by any State Party alleging that another has violated the Charter (*Articles 47 to 53*). The complaining State Party can submit its complaint first to the other State Party (*Article 47*). If the issue is not settled to the satisfaction of the two States Parties within three months of the complaint being received, either State Party may then submit the matter directly to the

Commission (*Article 48*). Alternatively, the State Party making the complaint may submit the matter directly to the Commission (*Article 49*). If an amicable solution cannot be reached, the Commission prepares a report stating the facts, its findings and any recommendations it wishes to make. These are sent to the States Parties concerned and to the OAU Assembly of Heads of State and Government.

- **Examination of Other Communications**
  The Commission may consider communications (complaints) from individuals and non-governmental organizations (*Articles 55 to 58*). The Commission considers such communications if a simple majority agrees that the complaints meet seven requirements (see pages 54 to 56). When it appears to the Commission that "one or more communications relate to special cases which reveal the existence of a series of serious or massive violations of human and peoples' rights, the Commission shall draw the attention of the OAU Assembly of Heads of State to these special cases" (*Article 58*). The Assembly "may then request the Commission to undertake an in-depth study of these cases and make a factual report, accompanied by its findings and recommendations" (*Article 58*). In emergency cases, the Chairperson of the Assembly may request the study. All measures taken under this procedure remain confidential until the Assembly decides to make them public (*Article 59*).

8 other provisions in the Charter

Articles 65, 66 and 68

The Charter takes effect for each new State Party three months after it deposits its instrument of ratification or accession to the Charter with the Secretary General of the OAU (*Article 65*).

The Charter may be supplemented by special protocols or agreements (*Article 66*). In addition, a simple majority of the States Parties may amend the Charter after all States Parties have been informed of the proposed amendment and the Commission has given its opinion at the request of the State Party proposing the amendment (*Article 68*).

In light of the dramatic changes in Africa since the Charter was adopted, several of those involved in drawing up the Charter have proposed that it should be amended. They have suggested strengthening the human rights guarantees in the Charter, such as allowing the Commission to publish its observations and conduct in-depth studies without seeking the permission of the OAU Assembly. They have also proposed the establishment of an African Court of Human and Peoples' Rights with the power to issue legally binding decisions. So far, however, no formal steps have been taken to amend the Charter.

A woman learning to write

9 how to make a complaint

WHO CAN MAKE A COMPLAINT?

Any individual or non-governmental organization, wherever they live or are based, may make a complaint, known as a "communication" (*Article 55*), to the African Commission concerning a violation by a State Party of one of the rights guaranteed by the African Charter. The author of the complaint can be any of the following:

- the victim of an alleged human rights violation by the government or officials of a state which has ratified the Charter
- a person or organization acting on the victim's behalf when the victim is unable to make the complaint
- an individual or organization alleging, with evidence, a series of serious or massive violations of human or peoples' rights

AGAINST WHOM CAN THE COMPLAINT BE MADE?

The complaint must be against a state which has ratified the Charter.

WHAT MUST BE IN THE COMPLAINT?

Complaints must satisfy seven requirements (*Article 56*). These are:

1. The complaint must indicate who is writing it. If the author is an individual, the complaint should indicate the name, address, age and profession. The author must be identified, even if the person does not want his or her name or organization known to the government of the state being complained about. The Commission will protect the anonymity of the author if requested to do so by the author.

2. The complaint must be compatible with the Charter of the OAU or the African Charter. The complaint must allege a violation by a State Party of a right or duty guaranteed by the Charter which took place after the Charter became legally binding on that State Party.

3. The complaint must not be written in disparaging or insulting language directed against the State concerned and its institutions or the OAU. It should simply state the facts and indicate how they constitute a violation of a right or duty protected by the Charter.

4. The complaint must not be based exclusively on information gathered from newspaper, radio or television reports. Part of it must be based on other sources such as personal knowledge, statements of witnesses or government documents (for example, legislation, decrees, court decisions or official gazettes).

5 The complaint must be sent after national remedies, if any, have been exhausted, unless it is obvious that these are unduly prolonged. The complaint should indicate which national remedies have been tried and the results. Although the Commission has not yet interpreted this provision, other treaty-monitoring bodies have held that if an appeal is pending in the national courts or the alleged victim has the right to appeal to a higher court, then national remedies have not been exhausted. If the remedy is discretionary — such as the right to seek pardon or commutation of a prison or death sentence — then it is possible that the Commission will decide that the remedy would not have to be used. It is likely that the Commission will decide that if the national remedy is likely to be futile then it need not be used.

6 The complaint must be submitted promptly after national remedies have been exhausted.

7 The complaint must not deal with cases which have been settled by the states involved in accordance with the principles of the UN Charter, the OAU's Charter or the African Charter. Complaints should not be about cases which have been or are being considered by another treaty-monitoring body such as the Human Rights Committee established under the International Covenant on Civil and Political Rights, or the Committee against Torture established under the Convention against Torture and

Other Cruel, Inhuman or Degrading Treatment or Punishment.

WHERE SHOULD THE COMPLAINT BE SENT?

The complaint should be sent to:

Secretary of the Commission,
African Commission on Human and Peoples' Rights,
Kairaba Avenue,
P.O.Box 673,
Banjul,
The Gambia

Telephone: (220) 92964
Telex : 2346 OAU BJL GV

WHAT HAPPENS TO THE COMPLAINT?

The Secretary of the Commission registers the complaint when it is received. Before each session, the registered complaints are sent by the Secretary to the members of the Commission.

The state concerned is given the chance to comment on whether the complaint against it is admissible. The Commission then decides by a simple majority whether the complaint satisfies the seven requirements in *Article 56* and therefore should be considered.

If the Commission decides that the complaint is inadmissible, it will promptly tell the author of the complaint and the State Party concerned. It may reconsider this decision if the author of the complaint writes again, showing that the grounds for deciding that the complaint was inadmissible no longer exist.

If the Commission decides that the complaint is admissible, it will inform the author and the State Party. The State Party must send a reply to the Commission within four months. This reply must explain the issues and indicate, if possible, any steps it has taken to remedy the situation. The Commission will send a copy of the reply to the author of the complaint, who may submit additional information and observations within a time limit fixed by the Commission.

The Commission will then consider the merits of the complaint in the light of all the information the author of the complaint and the State Party have submitted in writing. It then sends its observations on the complaint to the OAU Assembly, which may authorize the Commission to publish its observations.

When the Commission decides that "one or more communications apparently relate to special cases which reveal the existence of a series of serious or massive violations of human and peoples' rights", it informs the Assembly of Heads of State and Government. The Assembly may then ask the Commission to study these cases in greater depth and make a factual report, accompanied by its findings and recommendations. In emergencies, the Chairperson of the Assembly may request the in-depth study. The Commission will publish the report of the in-depth study after approval by the Assembly.

It is not yet clear how this procedure will work in practice because, as of the ninth ordinary session in March 1991, the Commission had not yet asked the OAU Assembly to publish its observations on any individual cases or asked it to conduct an in-depth study.

WHAT YOU CAN DO

1. Give copies of the Charter and this booklet to as many people as possible. Organize meetings or discussion groups to explain the rights and protections guaranteed by the Charter, particularly for those who cannot read it for themselves.

2. Show this booklet to anyone who wants to complain about a violation of their human rights to the African Commission.

3. Urge your government to ensure that the rights guaranteed in the Charter are upheld in your country in law and in practice. Make sure, also, that your government is fulfilling its obligations to submit its reports to the Commission every two years.

HOW TO ORDER COPIES OF THIS BOOKLET, THE AFRICAN CHARTER AND OTHER PUBLICATIONS ABOUT THE CHARTER

This booklet and copies of the African Charter in Arabic, English, French, Portuguese, Swahili and other African languages* are available from:

Amnesty International,
International Secretariat,
1 Easton Street,
London WC1X 8DJ,
United Kingdom

They are also available from the offices of Amnesty International sections and groups in Africa.

African Commission documents, including its annual activity reports and periodic reports of States Parties, are available from:

Secretary of the Commission,
African Commission on Human and Peoples' Rights,
Kairaba Avenue,
P. O. Box 673,
Banjul,
The Gambia

Telephone: (220) 92964
Telex : 2346 OAU BJL GV

**Copies in some of the languages may not be available until late 1991 or early 1992.*

selected articles from the African Charter

Article 1
The Member States of the Organization of African Unity parties to the present Charter shall recognize the rights, duties and freedoms enshrined in this Charter and shall undertake to adopt legislative or other measures to give effect to them.

Article 2
Every individual shall be entitled to the enjoyment of the rights and freedoms recognized and guaranteed in the present Charter without distinction of any kind such as race, ethnic group, colour, sex, language, religion, political or any other opinion, national and social origin, fortune, birth or other status.

Article 3
1. *Every individual shall be equal before the law.*
2. *Every individual shall be entitled to equal protection of the law.*

Article 4
Human beings are inviolable. Every human being shall be entitled to respect for his life and the integrity of his person. No one may be arbitrarily deprived of this right.

Article 5
Every individual shall have the right to the respect of the dignity inherent in a human being and to the recognition of his legal status. All forms of exploitation and degradation of man particularly slavery, slave trade, torture, cruel, inhuman or degrading punishment and treatment shall be prohibited.

Article 6
Every individual shall have the right to liberty and to the security of his person. No one may be deprived of his freedom except for reasons and conditions previously laid down by law. In particular, no one may be arbitrarily arrested or detained.

Article 7

1. *Every individual shall have the right to have his cause heard. This comprises:*

> *(a) The right to an appeal to competent national organs against acts violating his fundamental rights as recognized and guaranteed by conventions, laws, regulations and customs in force;*
>
> *(b) the right to be presumed innocent until proved guilty by a competent court or tribunal;*
>
> *(c) the right to defence, including the right to be defended by counsel of his choice;*
>
> *(d) the right to be tried within a reasonable time by an impartial court or tribunal.*

2. *No one may be condemned for an act or omission which did not constitute a legally punishable offence at the time it was committed. No penalty may be inflicted for an offence for which no provision was made at the time it was committed. Punishment is personal and can be imposed only on the offender.*

Article 8

Freedom of conscience, the profession and free practice of religion shall be guaranteed. No one may, subject to law and order, be submitted to measures restricting the exercise of these freedoms.

Article 9

1. *Every individual shall have the right to receive information.*
2. *Every individual shall have the right to express and disseminate his opinions within the law.*

Article 10

1. *Every individual shall have the right to free association provided that he abides by the law.*
2. *Subject to the obligation of solidarity provided for in Article 29 no one may be compelled to join an association.*

Article 11

Every individual shall have the right to assemble freely with others. The exercise of this right shall be subject only to necessary restrictions provided for by law in particular those enacted in the interest of national security, the safety, health, ethics and rights and freedoms of others.

Article 12

1. Every individual shall have the right to freedom of movement and residence within the borders of a State provided he abides by the law.

2. Every individual shall have the right to leave any country including his own, and to return to his country. This right may only be subject to restrictions, provided for by law for the protection of national security, law and order, public health or morality.

3. Every individual shall have the right, when persecuted, to seek and obtain asylum in other countries in accordance with the laws of those countries and international conventions.

4. A non-national legally admitted in a territory of a State Party to the present Charter, may only be expelled from it by virtue of a decision taken in accordance with the law.

5. The mass expulsion of non-nationals shall be prohibited. Mass expulsion shall be that which is aimed at national, racial, ethnic or religious groups.

Article 13

1. Every citizen shall have the right to participate freely in the government of his country, either directly or through freely chosen representatives in accordance with the provisions of the law.

2. Every citizen shall have the right of equal access to the public service of his country.

3. Every individual shall have the right of access to public property and services in strict equality of all persons before the law.

Article 14

The right to property shall be guaranteed. It may only be encroached upon in the interest of public need or in the general interest of the community and in accordance with the provisions of appropriate laws.

Article 15

Every individual shall have the right to work under equitable and satisfactory conditions, and shall receive equal pay for equal work.

Article 16

1. Every individual shall have the right to enjoy the best attainable state of physical and mental health.

2. States parties to the present Charter shall take the necessary measures to protect the health of their people and to ensure that they receive medical attention when they are sick.

Article 17

1. Every individual shall have the right to education.
2. Every individual may freely take part in the cultural life of his community.
3. The promotion and protection of morals and traditional values recognized by the community shall be the duty of the State.

Article 18

1. The family shall be the natural unit and basis of society. It shall be protected by the State which shall take care of its physical and moral health.
2. The State shall have the duty to assist the family which is the custodian of morals and traditional values recognized by the community.
3. The State shall ensure the elimination of every discrimination against women and also ensure the protection of the rights of the woman and the child as stipulated in international declarations and conventions.
4. The aged and the disabled shall also have the right to special measures of protection in keeping with their physical or moral needs.

Article 19

All peoples shall be equal; they shall enjoy the same respect and shall have the same rights. Nothing shall justify the domination of a people by another.

Article 20

1. All peoples shall have the right to existence. They shall have the unquestionable and inalienable right to self-determination. They shall freely determine their political status and shall pursue their economic and social development according to the policy they have freely chosen.
2. Colonized or oppressed peoples shall have the right to free themselves from the bonds of domination by resorting to any means recognized by the international community.
3. All peoples shall have the right to the assistance of the State parties to the present Charter in their liberation struggle against foreign domination, be it political, economic or cultural.

Article 21

1. *All peoples shall freely dispose of their wealth and natural resources. This right shall be exercised in the exclusive interest of the people. In no case shall a people be deprived of it.*

2. *In case of spoliation the dispossessed people shall have the right to the lawful recovery of its property as well as to an adequate compensation..*

3. *The free disposal of wealth and natural resources shall be exercised without prejudice to the obligation of promoting international economic co-operation based on mutual respect, equitable exchange and the principles of international law.*

4. *States parties to the present Charter shall individually and collectively exercise the right to free disposal of their wealth and natural resources with a view to strengthening African unity and solidarity.*

5. *States parties to the present Charter shall undertake to eliminate all forms of foreign economic exploitation particularly that practised by international monopolies so as to enable their peoples to fully benefit from the advantages derived from their national resources.*

Article 22

1. *All peoples shall have the right to their economic, social and cultural development with due regard to their freedom and identity and in the equal enjoyment of the common heritage of mankind.*

2. *States shall have the duty, individually or collectively, to ensure the exercise of the right to development.*

Article 23

1. *All peoples shall have the right to national and international peace and security. The principles of solidarity and friendly relations implicitly affirmed by the Charter of the United Nations and reaffirmed by that of the Organization of African Unity shall govern relations between States.*

2. *For the purpose of strengthening peace, solidarity and friendly relations, States parties to the present Charter shall ensure that:*

> *(a) any individual enjoying the right of asylum under Article 12 of the present Charter shall not engage in subversive activities against his country of origin or any other State party to the present Charter;*
>
> *(b) their territories shall not be used as bases for sub-*

versive or terrorist activities against the people of any other State party to the present Charter.

Article 24
All peoples shall have the right to a general satisfactory environment favourable to their development.

Article 25
States parties to the present Charter shall have the duty to promote and ensure through teaching, education and publication, the respect of the rights and freedoms contained in the present Charter and to see to it that these freedoms and rights as well as corresponding obligations and duties are understood.

Article 26
States parties to the present Charter shall have the duty to guarantee the independence of the Courts and shall allow the establishment and improvement of appropriate national institutions entrusted with the promotion and protection of the rights and freedoms guaranteed by the present Charter.

Article 27
1. *Every individual shall have duties towards his family and society, the State and other legally recognized communities and the international community.*
2. *The rights and freedoms of each individual shall be exercised with due regard to the rights of others, collective security, morality and common interest.*

Article 28
Every individual shall have the duty to respect and consider his fellow beings without discrimination, and to maintain relations aimed at promoting, safeguarding and reinforcing mutual respect and tolerance.

Article 29
The individual shall also have the duty:
1. *To preserve the harmonious development of the family and to work for the cohesion and respect of the family; to respect his parents at all times, to maintain them in case of need;*
2. *To serve his national community by placing his physical and intellectual abilities at its service;*
3. *Not to compromise the security of the State whose national or resident he is;*

__4.__ To preserve and strengthen social and national solidarity, particularly when the latter is threatened;
__5.__ To preserve and strengthen the national independence and the territorial integrity of his country and to contribute to its defence in accordance with the law;
__6.__ To work to the best of his abilities and competence, and to pay taxes imposed by law in the interest of the society;
__7.__ To preserve and strengthen the positive African cultural values in his relations with other members of the society, in the spirit of tolerance, dialogue and consultation and, in general, to contribute to the promotion of the moral well-being of society;
__8.__ To contribute to the best of his abilities, at all times and at all levels, to the promotion and achievement of African Unity.